I'm Thankful FOR you

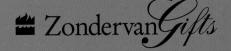
Zondervan Gifts

⛪ ZondervanPublishingHouse

Grand Rapids, Michigan 49530
http://www.zondervan.com

Senior Editor: Joy Marple
Project Editor: Sarah Hupp
Art Director: Robin Welsh
Designer: Christopher Tobias/Tobias Design
Illustrator: Erika LeBarre

Printed in China

Some quotations for this book were taken from the following:
Eleanor Doan, THE COMPLETE SPEAKERS SOURCEBOOK, Zondervan Publishing House, 1996; p. 3,5,8,9,23,29,45.
Robert I. Fitzhenry, ed., THE HARPER BOOK OF QUOTATIONS, 3rd ed., HarperPerennial, a division of HarperCollins Publishers, 1993; p. 32.
Frank S. Mead, ed., 12,000 RELIGIOUS QUOTATIONS, Baker Book House, 1989; p. 6,31, 32,36,39.
James Dalton Morrison, ed., MASTERPIECES OF RELIGIOUS VERSE, Baker Book House, 1977; p. 35,41.
George Sweeting, WHO SAID THAT?, Moody Press, 1995; p. 11,14,40,45.
R.E.O. White, YOU CAN SAY THAT AGAIN, Zondervan Publishing House, 1991; p. 31,34.

TO: "My Friend" - Jack Althouse

For all you've done and for all you mean to me — Thanks!

FROM:
Love in Christ
Hilda Quellbek

Dear Jack & Pat,

It's hard for me to put words on paper! You both at so special to me. Lifes takes us down so many different paths. But nothing the Lord says we can not handle. Jack you have

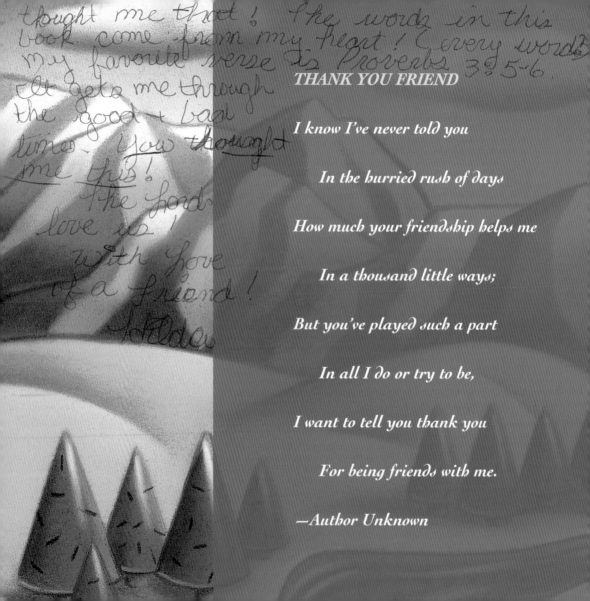

taught me that! The words in this
book come from my heart! Every word!
my favorite verse is Proverbs 3:5-6
It gets me through
the good + bad
times. You thought
me this!
The Lord
love us!
With Love
of a Friend!
Hilda

THANK YOU FRIEND

I know I've never told you

In the hurried rush of days

How much your friendship helps me

In a thousand little ways;

But you've played such a part

In all I do or try to be,

I want to tell you thank you

For being friends with me.

—Author Unknown

I thank my God every time I remember you.

–Philippians 1:3

Money and possessions may prove one wealthy;

but it is true friendship that makes one thankful.

—Sarah Michaels

I have not stopped giving thanks

for you, remembering you in my prayers.

—Ephesians 1:16

I'm thankful for the friendship
You give me every day.
I'm thankful for the love we share
Between us on life's way.
I'm thankful God sent you to me
To help my journey through;
But most of all I'm thankful that
You are you.

— Conover

A PRAYER OF THANKS

I thank you, God in Heaven, for friends.

When morning wakes, when daytime ends,

I have the consciousness of loving hands that touch my own,

of tender glance and gentle tone, of thoughts that cheer and bless!

—Margaret E. Sangster

Some things I am thankful for:

... that I do not have to be a cloud if I cannot be a star

... that only God and I know all the facts about me

... and that doors of opportunity are open before me because

friends like you help oil the hinges.

THANKS FOR A GOOD WORD

Each time we meet, you always have

    Some word of praise that makes me glad.

You see some hidden, struggling trait,

    Encourage it and make it great.

My day takes on a brand-new zest.

    Your gift of praising brings my best,

Revives my spirit, flings it high;

    For God loves praise, and so do I.

—Author Unknown

I'm grateful to you for being a friend who will

strengthen others with your prayers, bless others with your love,

and encourage others with your hope.

The joy that you give to others

Is the joy that comes back to you.

—John Greenleaf Whittier

I SAID A PRAYER

I said a prayer for you today

And know God must have heard;

I felt the answer in my heart

Though he spoke not a word.

I asked for happiness for you

In all things great and small;

But that you'd know his loving care

I prayed the most of all.

—Author Unknown

I thank God . . . as night and day

I constantly remember you in my prayers.

−2 Timothy 1:3

I always thank my God as I
remember you in my prayers.
—Philemon 4

Thank you for the friendship you give me,
for accepting me for myself
and not for what you could help me become
or for what you thought I could be;
but for what I am now,
this very moment.
For friendship and acceptance and understanding,
I thank you.
—Conover

Every good and perfect gift is from

above, coming down from the Father

of the heavenly lights, who does not

change like shifting shadows.

—James 1:17

A FRIEND LIKE YOU

When it's cloudy outside, I have sun in my day

Because of a friend like you.

When my purse holds no coin, I'm still richer than kings

Because of a friend like you.

Friends like you share the good times.

Friends like you share the tough times;

And all in-between times too.

And though I don't say it as oft' as I should

I'm glad for a friend like you.

—Sarah Michaels

My friend, you make the world a more beautiful place to be, and for that I am truly thankful.

Give thanks in all circumstances.
—1 Thessalonians 5:18

In everything give thanks to God . . .
And this is what I do.
Every day I thank the Lord
For such a friend as you.
—Conover

Being thankful for friends is a guarantee of contentment.

ONE WHO SOWS COURTESY, REAPS FRIENDSHIP;

ONE WHO PLANTS KINDNESS, GATHERS LOVE;

AND THE ONE WHO PRACTICES GOOD DEEDS,

GATHERS THANKFULNESS BY THE BUSHEL.

–AFTER BASIL

We always thank God for all of you, mentioning you
in our prayers.
— 1 Thessalonians 1:2

A COMFORTING THOUGHT

There's a comforting thought at the close of the day
 When I'm weary and lonely and sad,
That sort of grips hold of my crusty old heart
 And bids it be merry and glad.
It gets in my soul and drives out the blues,
 And finally thrills through and through.
It is just a sweet memory that chants the refrain:
 "I'm glad for good friends just like you!"
—Anonymous

A generous man will prosper; he who refreshes
others will himself be refreshed.
—Proverbs 11:25

Every sincere word of forgiveness we ever speak is a word of God; every generous deed is a service to God's kingdom; and every expression of thanks is a recognition of God's love bestowed through another.

Your love has given me great joy and encouragement.
—Philemon 7

Every day I pray for God to bless you as you have blessed me, my friend. And I thank him for your gift of friendship's shared joys and sorrows. You are in my heart, my thoughts, my prayers . . . you are my friend.

Friends are like snowflakes . . . it's amazing what happens when we stick together!

Let shadows come,
        Let shadows go;
Let life be bright
        Or full of woe.
I am content,
        For this I know:
Thou thinkest, Friend, of me.
        —Anonymous

Thank you for that wonderful moment

when our minds touched;

our hearts overlapped;

and our souls bonded.

For being part of my life;

touching my life;

enriching my life;

thank you.

— Conover

[I] always thank God, the Father of our
Lord Jesus Christ, . . . for you.
—Colossians 1:3

You help me see the visions in my mind more clearly.

You help me define who I am.

I'm so glad God sent you to be my friend.

—Conover

Constantly I remember you in my prayers at all times.

—Romans 1:9–10

May God grant you a wonderful blessing to make

your day a joyful one . . . for you are a joy to me.

I'M THANKFUL YOU'VE SPURRED ME ON TO

GRATEFUL LIVING, FOR PEOPLE WHO ARE

GRATEFUL ARE DRIVEN TO HELP OTHERS JUST

AS THEY HAVE BEEN HELPED THEMSELVES.

You have filled my heart with greater joy.

—Psalm 4:7a

Father, I thank you for the gift of friendship;
for this one whose heart shares my joys and
sorrows, this one who keeps the light of
hope ever burning before my wandering
steps, this one who accepts me for what I am
and for what I am not. May this special one
see your light in the darkest night and
glimpse your love reflected in me. Amen.

Thankfulness for one's friends finds itself manifest in three forms:

a strong feeling in the heart, a warm expression of grateful words,

and a willing generosity to share with others in return.

The LORD bless you and keep you; the LORD make his face shine upon you and be gracious to you; the LORD turn his face toward you and give you peace.

—Numbers 6:24–26

Thankfulness for a friend is born when one takes time to count up past kindnesses.

Thankfulness is a language which the
blind can see and the deaf can hear.

You always let me blow off steam
And don't condemn me for it.
And when I've made a huge mistake
You kindly will ignore it.
You let me be just who I am
Right now, this very day.
God bless you, my special friend.
I'm glad you came my way.
—Conover

I thank my God through Jesus Christ for . . . you.
—Romans 1:8

Friendship is a chain of gold

   Shaped in God's all perfect mold.

Each link a smile, a laugh, a tear,

   A grip of the hand, a word of cheer.

Steadfast as the ages roll

   Binding closer soul to soul;

No matter how far or heavy the load

   Sweet is the journey on friendship's road.

Let the peace of Christ rule in your hearts. . . . And be thankful.
—Colossians 3:15

THE PEERLESS BOND OF FRIENDSHIP

BETWEEN US IS SO STRONG.

AND I GIVE THANKS TO GOD EACH DAY

BECAUSE YOU CAME ALONG.

Oh, the comfort, the inexpressible comfort of feeling safe with a

person, having neither to weigh thoughts, nor measure words, but

pouring them all right out — just as they are, chaff and grain

together — certain that a faithful hand will take and sift them . . .

keep what is worth keeping . . . and with the breath of kindness

blow the rest away.

— Dinah Maria Mulock Craik

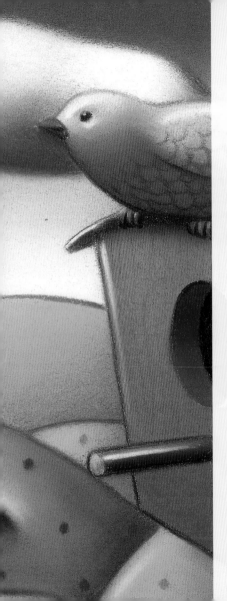

I'm thankful for your cheerful words;

    Appreciate your smile;

I'm pleased you are considerate—

    No one would you revile.

I'm grateful for your humor,

    And your humility;

But most of all I'm thankful that

    You've been a friend to me.

—Sarah Michaels

Always giving thanks to God the Father for

everything, in the name of our Lord Jesus Christ.

—Ephesians 5:20

For all the blessings of the year,

For all the friends we hold so dear,

For peace on earth, both far and near,

We thank thee, Lord.

–ALBERT H. HUTCHINSON

May the Lord show kindness to you, as you have shown . . . to me.

—Ruth 1:8

God,

Thank you for the gift of laughter.

Thank you for the sorrows shared.

Thank you for the loving heart

In this friend who always cares.

Amen.

—Conover

May he give you the desire of your heart and make all your plans succeed.

—Psalm 20:4

Be careful for nothing;

Be prayerful for anything;

Be thankful for everything.

—Dwight L. Moody

I'm grateful that you share my sadness and my happiness, friend.

A sorrow shared is half a trouble,

but joy that's shared is joy made double.

—Anonymous

A person can make a difference in

relationships and make the world

a more beautiful place by just saying

"Thank you." What joy is enfolded

in those two simple words.

God is pleased with no music below as much as with

the songs of rejoicing, comforted and thankful persons.

—Jeremy Taylor

Little charities fly furthest and stay longest on the wing

when they are accompanied with a word of thanks.

A THANKFUL FRIEND IS A GIVING FRIEND . .

.ONE WHO HAS LEARNED THAT GIVING IS

THE REAL PURPOSE OF LIVING.

None is so rich or mighty that he can get along

without a word of thanks and none is so poor that

he cannot be made rich by it. Yet thankfulness

cannot be bought, begged, borrowed or stolen,

for it is something that is of no value to anyone

unless it is given freely.